Real Stories from a Rideshare Driver

Scott Cvek

The Becand Group
Elizabethtown, PA
2020

The Becand Group
Elizabethtown, PA 17022 USA

ISBN 9781787233102

FORWARD

Real Stories from real people is the premise of this book. From hard luck stories to funny stories to interesting stories, they are all very real to the passengers I've driven over the last two years. These riders were kind enough to share them with me, and for that, I am grateful.

I drive in a small town that is situated between three medium sized cities, so my experiences have been slightly different than a driver who works in a large city, by giving, on average, 5-10 minute rides. Mine were mostly 10-20 minute rides, which allows for more conversation and dialogue between the driver and the passenger(s).

I've given over 4,300 rides for more than 2 years; I've had many experiences with driving for the two major ridesharing companies. Many of them were good, some of them not so good and most of them in between. This book includes those stories that reflect the idea that everyone has a story. If anyone feels that their story is the worst, or the best, they are wrong.

George

Bike Rider, Home to Friends' House

He rode 11 miles, and then his bike broke down. He informed me about some local trails and other outdoor activities in the area. Hearing from a local who actively participates is the best way to hear about things to do.

Lisa

Home to Work at Starbucks

Needed a ride to work, commented about slow customers who order coffee and have no idea what to order. Also, no free coffee for employees, but they do try samples from the selections they put out for customers.

Spencer

Home to Vet

This young lady, a transplant from a local city, was taking her cat to get spayed. I learned a lot about cats and kittens on this 20 minute ride. Also, we discussed about the differences of urban and rural people, generally speaking. I wished her well, living outside of a city and quite frankly, a slightly different way of living. Later, learned she tipped $10.00, very nice.

Amanda with daughter

Department Store to Home

Having young children in the vehicle made me realize that I needed to have something for them, besides the usual amenities. In this case, I offered some butterscotch hard candies to Ana, the daughter. And, after some bantering and kidding back and forth with this Kindergarten aged daughter, she was having fun. And even more than that, while exiting my car, she quipped, 'I hope we have you as our driver again', and she thanked me for the candy. And coming from a young child, you know it's sincere; the comment made my day.

Mike

Hotel to Train Station to Wedding

He is from South Jersey & Staten Island; he has never been to Ellis Island, which is kind of funny, but so true for many people when they live near a famous landmark, etc., they tend not to go there. Only customer I know who has experienced two losses from the 9/11 tragedy. And, he also has not been to the 9/11 memorial. That's understandable. But, he has been to some local events, such as the Falmouth Goat Races, a small town get together.

Talik
Home to Work

He talked like an older person, mature for his age, he's only 21. I commented about his unique name and stated he does know 3 other people named Talik. I'm not sure where he's from, should have asked. Didn't expect tip, but later learned he tipped $3.00.

Austin
Gas Station to Home

Seeing three guys standing around outside of mini-market, smoking cigarettes, etc; one of them was Austin. First impression was not a positive one, but as is often the case, I was wrong. Well, at least for now. He spoke of moving away from a large city, partly because he just served 2 years in a state penitentiary and wanted to 'start over'. With a wife and a child, he's struggling to find employment, but is still confident he doesn't want to go back to prison. He spoke of being homeless with his family and sleeping in a public park. Not easy to imagine for many people, but I empathize with him, wish him well, and I say a prayer for him after he leaves the vehicle.

Tenny
Hotel to Train Station

Very nice Taiwanese lady, traveled to the area for an Asian Conference. Another example of the international influence from our local College, which most people do not know about.

Jennifer with 2 small dogs
Walking Trail to Home

This rider let me know after I accepted the ride, that she had two dirty dogs. So, I brought a towel for the back seat. They were small dogs and not that dirty but I appreciated the text letting me know ahead of time. Turns out she works 6 days, 10 hours a day for a few months over the holiday season. Some drivers might turn down this ride, but I typically do not. Mostly, it could mean a nice tip and that's what happened. And my vehicle did not get dirty either.

Driver Thoughts

Sometimes when you pick up or drop off a customer, it's not the safest or the most convenient, etc.

In one case, with a train station terminal being under construction, with it raining and cold outside, and with an hour wait for the train, there was no indoor area to wait. So, I drove around the station and did find a place for her to wait. However, before doing that I finished the ride on the app, so she didn't pay extra for the experience. Then, as sometimes happens when you are nice, she left a tip. And, keep in mind that drivers get 100% of all tips, both cash and on the app.

Unfortunately, many people don't realize that being an UBER/Lyft driver is, in some ways, similar to a waiter/waitress. If a customer tips little or not at all when going to a restaurant, they probably don't tip their ride share driver either. The difference is that in a restaurant, a person knows exactly what they pay for the meal and the tip amount. In the driving world, people don't see how little the driver actually gets from the fare, which has been decreasing since these ridesharing services began.

Susan

Work to Dr. Office Visit

Nice person, but not talkative, for some reason. Not a problem, though, it happens. This was a 16 minute ride with very little conversation, some people just don't want to talk and/or they are not in the mood.

Bran with wife and 5th grade son

Motel to school district

Family is on its way to registering their son in a new school district, in the middle of the year. Tough family situation, some details given and with enough details to feel and hope for the best for each of them, especially the son. I wished them well and good luck.

Hillary & friend

Home to Sports Bar

Both were wearing NFL Giants football Jersey's so I spoke about the game today between them and the Eagles. They said they are going to the game in

Philly. I made it known that they are either very brave or crazy to do that. They thought it was a funny thought, but they didn't understand that although it may be funny, it is a very real thing to not wear your 'team colors' when going to a Philadelphia sports team event in Philly. Of course, only when you are the visiting team. They'll find out why soon enough.

Robin

Hotel to department store

She was on the phone the whole time. Speaking to her father about still giving money to her and her siblings, and loudly, which is why I hear the conversation. She is in her mid 30's. Dad is currently paying over $900 weekly for her to stay in a hotel until she finds a permanent place to live. Sometimes it's hard to understand certain situations, but obviously, there is more to the story, but I'm confident it's quite a story and probably one I would find difficult to understand.

Jon

Friend's house to Business

He is the owner/operator of a local glass business that specializes in locally made blown glassware for smoking different things. He dresses and talks like an old rock group follower. Currently has 5 employees and has been in business about 10 years. First glance of business from outside looks shady, but after seeing the inside, it's truly legit. Once again, looks can be deceiving; it's that 'don't judge a book by its cover' thing.

Andrea & friend

Home to friend's home

This was not a typical ride. Andrea entered the vehicle as a friendly person, starting a conversation right away. She is a music teacher at a local school and the topic of racism was raised. It is best to avoid such topics, to avoid possible verbal confrontations. She was born and raised on the West coast, so her views differ from many of her friends, etc. She has a good soul, represented by her working as an EMT as well. Although it was a civil conversation, it could have turned out much differently; so it is still best to avoid it as much as possible and to keep the subject matter as light as possible.

Valerie

Home to friend's house & back home

Having relocated from a big city to a rural area, Valerie would seem to be out of her element.

However, her disposition and personality most definitely overshadows any challenges that come her way. And by challenges, I mean life changing events. She was a victim of what seemed at first as a drive by shooting, and later turned out that she was targeted to teach a lesson to her boyfriend. When finding this out, she broke up and left the city. Bringing her three adult children and their families was the plan, but only the son decided, so far, to move with her. In spite of her experience of lying on a sidewalk, being close to death from a gunshot wound, she still wakes up every day with a positive attitude towards the coming day. She obviously does not play the 'victim' card and is moving on in life.

Harley

Home to Mom's Home

A short trip, but she requests to stop at a mini market. She comes out with a half dozen donuts to feed 4 young girls that her mom is babysitting. As she said, 'I'm sugaring them up'. A conversation ensues about giving loud, noise making toys to relatives' children, to be funny, of course.

Amber

Friends house to pick up car from last night

No, I did not pick up Amber. I picked up some guy, not sure of his name. There are many times when you pick up someone, they are not the ones on the phone app or paying for the ride. But, the rider usually knows the payer, could be a family member or a friend or sometimes a bar owner, etc. In this case, the rider didn't even know who Amber was, kinda funny. From a driver's perspective, you still get paid, so it really doesn't matter all that much. It ended up being a good ride financially. I got the normal fare from Amber, about $10 and I got a $10 tip from the rider who was most appreciative of me offering a bottle of water to him.

Jil (Correct Spelling)

Train Station to Hotel

This was my first ride for a citizen of England; specifically, Manchester, England. She was a nice person who missed her train stop and arrived locally, needing to be driven about 30 minutes away. She made the book because of her not being a soccer (football) sports fan, while being from Manchester, England. This is weird because Manchester is home to two of the most successful soccer teams in the world and every weekly match is at least as big a deal as an NFL football playoff game, at least to the locals.

Daniel

Home to Haircut and later back Home

I picked up Daniel, in his 50's; at his home; he had a white, folding blind stick, so I assumed his eyesight was very bad. As it turned out, he was born blind, has worked for many years, retired from a government job for the state. He mentioned that he retired early due to, what he perceived, as discrimination. He was my first totally blind passenger, and I can't imagine going through life not ever seeing anything. I'm not sure how he even managed to request a ride. After some conversation, he mentioned that, certainly, at times, people do take advantage of him because he cannot see, that is heartbreaking. Basically, he has challenges every day of his life, and obviously, he has overcome and/or dealt with them with some success. His story could take up many pages and after dropping him off, I wanted to speak and learn more about his trials and tribulations and also to do more for him.

Howard

Train Station to Medical Center

This is a frequent rider that may have multiple entries throughout the book. Howard is a cardiologist with an intellect that far outweighs his physical capabilities. Although he struggles to get around, his insight and our conversations typically leave me with new and interesting thoughts about many different aspects of life and the world around us. This ride was no different. Howard is from a city of about 5 million people and one point of our conversation today was how a nearby metropolis of about 16 million people has seen people move from there to a smaller city that he lives, with about 5 million people. I mentioned that in our small, rural area, we see a number of folks moving from the 5 million people city to an area with less than ½ million people. It's all relative, in that, it depends what you are used to and how you have been programmed to live. It's not necessarily a good or bad thing, but the idea of a living in a bubble, can create the reality of both your physical surroundings as well as your mental outlook on the world around us.

Frances

Train Station to Home

This story is absolutely true, almost unbelievable, but true.

She was born and raised in a big city, later moving to a very southern state because of marriage and having a son. While going through a divorce, her home burns down. The ex-husband asks her to move nearby for the son's sake. He gets remarried and offers for her to stay at his new place till she gets her own place. After a while, Frances finds out the real reason he wanted her to stay there. It turns out the ex-husband wanted some loving 'on the side'.

Then she proceeds to inform me that at this moment in time, she is on her way to a large disagreement and she mentions, 'I'm going to kill him'. I kiddingly say that I hope not or law enforcement may have to get involved. Then she tells me that the local authorities already know her as she recently had an altercation with them.

So, I then mention the book and I tell her that I'll change her name, but would like to use her story. She says, 'no, don't change my name'. And she goes on to say that she is writing a book about her life's adventures, so of course, I encourage that.

I wish her well and proceed to say a prayer for her.

Lauren

Sister's House to Brother's House

A crying and emotional passenger first thing in the morning is not a great thing for a driver, but it is not our choice. Boyfriend breaking up with her, etc.. Fortunately I carry small packets of Kleenex with sandwich bags so customers can use them and have some place to put them. Lauren definitely used them, but she wanted more from me, like empathy and a solution to her situation. I offered some advice with empathy as well, but definitely not one of my strengths. I used the phrase, 'time heals all wounds' and hoped that soon that will make sense to her.

Marie Claire

Home to Business

She and her fiancé have a small business in the bio-chemical world. Both of them are Bio-Chemists and have taken out their savings to begin a new company. Already with a few good contracts, they may very well be on their way to financial freedom. It's amazing to see two well educated and young (28 and 29 years old) people take that leap of faith to make it happen.

Driver Thoughts

When going to pick up a rider, there is always the potential issue of them sitting up front, in the passenger seat.

Typically, I have my water bottle cooler on the seat, but some people just wait till you move it. Others see it, and go in the back seat, sitting where you can see them by a slight turn of the head. Some riders sit directly behind you. I asked one person why and also explained to them that it is sort of unnerving when they sit there. They went on to explain that they had a bad experience with a previous driver, so they always sit there. I respect that, but it is still awkward.

And, speaking of bad experiences, I've heard of many stories of rides that were 'challenging' for the passenger, and later in this book I speak of some of them.

However, when picking up females for a ride, I almost always speak of the safety measures that are in place on each of the apps. Unfortunately, many were not aware of them. They include; sharing your ride and the '911' button. If you are not aware of these, then please check them out before your next ride. It is a necessary safety measure, especially when you are in a strange place, riding alone, or riding at night.

Sierra

Home to Eye Doctor

21 year old Sierra has a rare disease, three long medical terms that I do not remember. Simply put, her vertebrae is producing excess water, that in turn is settling in her head, creating 'water in the brain', not a good thing. So rare, there is not a lot of research going on and it is still quite a mystery, creating excessive and long-lasting migraines that are immune to normal drugs. On any given day, she could go completely blind, or worse. Symptoms can come and go, without any notice. I concurred with her that her Christmas wishes are different than the average person and I also mentioned that I would say a prayer for her, her husband and two children.

Theresa

Home to Friends House – Long Ride

Typically the long rides that I am involved in are very conversational, amusing, interesting, etc. This ride was one of those times. Being a horse trainer, Theresa knew a lot about the caretaking and training of horses along with providing much information about the horse racing industry. She explained how most horse owners in the horse racing industry are very insensitive about the well being of the animals, especially after their racing years are over. Many people have strong feelings about what they are passionate about, and that was the case with Theresa. It can be important to listen more when taking rides, it's good for the soul and it's good for tips, most times.

Juan

Home to Inner city

An admitted ex-convict, 25 years old, with 4 years left on probation, needed a ride to walk around a new city. Coming from a much larger city, Philadelphia, he has experienced quite a bit for someone his age. Unfortunately most of those experiences were not good; including being shot six different times, seeing other people get murdered and even more people over-dosing on drugs. His willingness to deal drugs and participate in other illegal activities, just to make some easy money has led him to serve some time in prison. Fortunately for him, he has seen the light and knows now that there is another way to live. Not everyone ever gets to find this out. He is now employed, already got a raise, does not associate with his previous friends and very much likes living in a rural area where, in his words, 'People care about each other.' A great story to tell other people and that's exactly what I spoke with him about…

Fred
Home to Friend's House

An interesting and non-descript fellow entered my vehicle not saying much and not moving with a purpose. As he sat quietly, not answering any attempt for small talk, I noticed a fly on my window. After realizing it was inside the car I decided to roll the window down to let it escape. Having done this and rolling the window up, I mentioned to Fred why I was opening and closing the window. I said either the fly left the vehicle or got blown back in by the wind, no response from him. After a few seconds, I glance back and see him holding the fly between his two fingers and very quietly and unemotionally quipped, 'I got him', he opened the back window and let him out. No other comment or expression of accomplishment, so it was kind of strange, obviously a lot more going on in his head that was not understandable to me. I kept quiet and only laughed to myself, thinking that I tell people all of the time, it's a no judgment zone.

John

Downtown store to Mini Market to Home

He was just another passenger, until he got in the car and I realized he could not speak or hear anything and almost totally blind, lost those abilities shortly after birth. Not knowing sign language, I wrote down my questions on paper and he responded as such. Having worked in a government job for over 20 years, he felt he was being discriminated against by a certain boss and decided to retire. We joked and he grew comfortable and very appreciative of my regular conversation with him, he offered to buy me lunch at the mini-market, I declined. Typically, I avoid accepting these offers, for a host of reasons. After conversing a few more times, I stopped at his residence, saw him use his cane to measure his distant to his front door, found out he can see light but most everything is hazy and not clear. He spoke about how a home contractor tried to take advantage of him because of his handicaps and I empathized with his plight. After closing the car door and driving away I said a prayer for him and hoped for the best. This was definitely one of those times when I wanted to do more for him; it can be an ongoing issue with a driver that has a heart, apparently I do, at least sometimes.

Driver Thoughts

There are numerous actions a driver can take to make each trip an enjoyable one for the passenger(s).

The right temperature, good music that's not too loud, a clean car, free mints and/or water bottles are some positive actions. Although doing all of these does not guarantee a tip, it certainly can increase the odds. Unfortunately, for those drivers whose average ride is less than 10 minutes, tips are less frequent.

Many passengers think the driver gets the whole fare or at least they don't understand that a $10 fare typically only means $3 or $4 for the driver. Although it's a similar understanding with longer rides, many times the fare issue for drivers can be explained diplomatically without directly coming out and saying, 'Tips are accepted and most appreciated'.

But, it's not always about the tip. I've given 'free' rides to those passengers, who are in a tough time in their life and just need to get somewhere. This is one of those times when I am reminded just how blessed and lucky that I am. It is also a good time to be more grateful and to not take everything for granted, even the simple day to day things, like family and friends.

Michelle

Home to Work

Same as many regular work rides, but a little different. Working at a local Subway, which is locally owned and operated, her boss pays for the UBER ride to and from work, and not just her but other workers who need the service as well. And this happens on a regular basis. It turns out that it is one of the perks to get and keep good employees. First time I've heard of this, but only a small price to pay to help keep good and reliable workers in a high turnover job.

Yvette & Mom (69yrs old)

Drs. Office to Hotel

Yvette walks her mom, Carol, out to the car, slowly but surely. She goes back into the office to get some paperwork she had forgotten. In the meantime, I offer Carol a bottle of water and I open it for her. She is shaking and starts to spill it on herself a little bit. I then joke with her, saying, 'I'm not driving until you put the cap back on', saying this so she doesn't continue to spill it all over herself. She laughs and says, 'You are too funny'.

So, I offer her a life saver mint and she begins to chew it immediately. I joke again, saying, 'You are supposed to suck on them, not chew them'. She laughs again. At this point, I figure this is going to be an interesting ride.

Well, the daughter returns and I soon find out that Carol has full blown dementia, and the daughter is taking care of her full time. Suddenly, the realization of my busy life seems inconsequential compared to this life situation. Although this episode was somewhat hilarious, I can only imagine the long days and overall story of both passengers.

Lorianne

Home to Department Store

A middle age, generally pleasant woman who requests multiple short rides, which means a small fare for the driver. She complains about drivers cancelling rides for her on a regular basis. I explain that because she lives in a town of only about twelve thousand people, there are not a lot of drivers. That means, when requested, they need to come from at least 15-20 minutes away. It also means that the driver, getting only $3 or $4 for all that driving, may not want to come that distance and lose money.

I do it, because I live in a similar small town and I understand the plight of middle aged and older people needing rides, even if it's a low fare. Getting older myself; it appeals to the empathetic side of me.

Arty
Home to Car

Another smart passenger who was out partying and realized he had been drinking too much and left his car at the bar. It's kind of humorous how many rides are given to return people to their vehicle from the night before. Sometimes, they don't know exactly where the vehicle is, so we drive around until it's found. Of course, I only snicker about this to myself, because I drive a 'No Judgment UBER/Lyft'. This driver, however, wanted me to give him ideas for a wedding gift that he is attending later this evening. Not quite prepared, so I do my best with some last minute ideas. I try to only give my opinion when directly asked for it or if it matches the opinion of the passenger. It's just a good idea; after all, I am providing a service, so it should be a positive experience.

Robin
Bed/breakfast to a Wedding

I was certainly honored to drive a preacher to oversee an actual wedding for the day. Being from out of town, I offer some local historical information, etc. She is responsive to the info, but then proceeds to ask me, like so many others, is driving very profitable? The answer is that, it depends. For me, it's mostly profitable because it fits my business plan. I mention how many drivers only last a short time due to not treating it as a personal business; with goals, a plan and the willingness to put the effort into adapting to where they live and how it can fit into their lives. I also mention that it's more than money for me, it's actually very therapeutic. It's a great way to bring up the idea that everyone has a story. She is interested in purchasing and puts the website into her phone for future usage. This is another ride where I wish it was longer to get more of her thoughts and opinions, etc.

Makaela

Friend's house to Home

She is a nice person and we had good conversation on a 15 minute ride. One thing she mentioned that I thought was kind of funny. She mentioned that she just moved to the area. Also, no children just two dogs to take care of. She works 5 or 6 ten hour days per week, so she has the dogs go to a doggie day care; that actually picks up the dogs in the morning and returns them in the afternoon. So she goes on to mention how some parents look for a house in a good school district, etc. and that she actually looked for a house within the pick-up radius for her doggie day care. Kind of funny, but she needs to work long hours and wanted the dogs to get taken care of beyond her coming home for lunch during the day. In her story, the dogs mean everything to her.

Ashley

Campground to a Pharmacy

Picked up a 30 something whose getting her car back from the garage in a about a week, so she needed an UBER for a few days. She lives locally and has used the campground as a low cost getaway for her family and children over the years. She has also been divorced but is soon going to be married again. This time at the campground it's her personal getaway, her personal time, to re-focus her life and get some real quiet time alone. It's something almost every person's story could use from time to time.

John

Airport to Home

This was a story of another all too common theme in the world today. Married for 19 years, with an 18 month old daughter, his wife decided she wanted a 'life reset', and is leaving him. Although mostly a quiet ride, after he fell asleep, he did say one thing that made me think about my own story, in a sad way. After mentioning to him how blessed he is to have a daughter, he said, 'Yes, she definitely has a piece of my heart'.

Kaylin

Friends House to Home

Once in a while, I pick up a young person who seems to have it all together. A 17 year old young man, from a very large city, moved to this area (a small, rural town) as a youngster. Joining the Air Force in a few weeks, he has detailed plans of what he'll be doing during and after his military commitment. He excelled in high school despite losing his father to incarceration at an early age. Him and his 5 other siblings were raised by his mother and grandmother. His appreciation and respect for these two women was certainly understood and appreciated by him and he didn't hesitate to give them many accolades. I'm only imagining what I was thinking and doing at 17, certainly not acting like this. What a great and hopeful story.

Mary Jo

Home to Drug Store and back Home

A friendly, elderly lady, ordered a ride through the GoGoGrandparents app.(This is an app for people with flip phones). I turned on the Frank Sinatra station on the radio and she loved it. She spoke of how when she was a youngster her friends created a club called the 'Society for the Swooney Souls of the Sensational Sinatra'. Because they all loved him so much, they even learned how to write cursive the same way as Frank. Their love for him is probably not much different than any other generational love for a musical band. Also, as happens on many a ride, she recommended I try a certain brand of cinnamon tea. She went on and on how it was getting difficult to find this product anywhere. I suspect she very much appreciated our conversation throughout the stops and thus, that is one of the main reasons I typically drive in a more rural area than a big city.

Xvaria

Home to Work

This was another nice person who wanted to talk about some other driver experiences, especially after hearing about my book being written. One recent ride had her with multiple stops. After the first stop, the driver informed her that he didn't want to go that far and proceeded to end the ride and drove away. Another driver did the same thing, except in this case, there was no conversation; he just drove off after the first stop. It amazes me that this behavior actually happens, but I believe there are drivers who just don't get the customer service part of this operation.

Sarah

Home to Mom's house

A 19ish young lady that seems troubled in more ways than I'll ever know; she has a definite attitude. This quickly came across in her conversation; feeling as though the world owes her something. Like all rides, this is just a brief moment in the riders' life and is not always indicative of a person's normal behavior. I'm hoping this is the case with Sarah, and that she is normally a nice person.

Liz

Home to a Pizza restaurant

She is a 22 year old young lady who is meeting friends at a pizza place for lunch. I quickly realize that she thinks and talks like an older, more mature person. Recently, she broke up with a boy who is still acting out his high school years. She mentions that he is still just into video games, TV binge watching, etc. and that she is ready to live and experience the world around us. Certainly a mature thought for a young person, but very refreshing to hear.

Mike
Train station to his old college

He is a recent college graduate coming back to his roots for a job fair. He is a very young person mentally, with many life experiences still awaiting him. He does recognize that the job he is in now is not a long term solution for him, and that's more than some people his age are able to realize. I wish him good luck in his search for the perfect job. His story is in here as a reminder when life was simpler and less complicated.

Rachael (w/husband and another couple)
Hotel to Wedding

Four out of town people dressed up and going to a wedding, they expressed the thought that they were late, so I'm driving with a purpose. It's a fifteen minute ride, so time to converse about where there from, etc. Also, time to provide them some historical and current info about the area. Most people appreciate it and many people enjoy hearing this info from a local person. As we approach the wedding venue, people are filing out of the church. I didn't realize that they were actually about 30 minutes late and had missed the wedding, but just in time for the reception. Being a high priced wedding, over

$15,000, it was a bit awkward for them getting out of the car as the bride steps out of the church, only about 20 feet away. I withhold my laughter, until driving away from the scene. Hopefully, they bought them a nice gift or lots of money.

Lawrence

Work to Home to Work

I picked up an ex-Marine and his bicycle. I didn't know I could fit a bike completely inside a Ford Focus hatchback. He normally rides his bike to his first job, a one hour and 15 minute trek. Then, he rides it home, just in time to go to his second place of employment. So, for all those people who say they need a car to get to work, he is proof that where there is a will, there is a way. This day, however, he was pressed for time, thus the rideshare request. Currently raising a family and doing what is necessary to make ends meet, his military background has prepared him well. He just graduated college and is moving up in the world. I thanked him for his service to our country and wished him well.

Driver Thoughts

One common story I've heard is about driver's talking about their own personal issues.

This is not recommended in most trips for many reasons. Many people are very much into their own situation and are not very interested in hearing about a stranger's issues in life, especially when they are paying to be in a rideshare situation. It's best to listen twice as much as you speak, you'll find that most times it can be very comforting to a rider. There are many lonely people in the world as well as many people who have no one around them to empathize and not judge their own ideas and/or actions in life. It does take practice to listen and try to understand their outlook as they view it. It's a good attribute as a driver as well in life.

Some other issues with driver stories have been: loud or obnoxious music, smoky car, dirty inside the car, not being able to speak English.

One disturbing story was when the driver offered three young people to look in the glove compartment, if they are really looking for a good time. Inside were needles, syringes, heroin, etc. Fortunately, the passengers asked him to pull over and they got out. It's amazing, just amazing that this driver may still be out there.

Stephanie

Relative's Home to Airport

This was a long ride, 1 ½ hours, and she had plenty to talk about. Early on in my rideshare experience, this was my longest ride to date. As it turned out, this was a great learning experience for me to listen and be a sounding board for a multitude of family issues and struggles. She asked that I not mention the details in this book, so I won't. But I can say that all families have some issues at least some of the time. Sometimes those issues are not as open to anyone outside of the family, but rest assured they do exist for everyone.

Paul

Home to Work (Repeat Customer)

A very nice guy with a good job and chooses to use ridesharing on a regular basis to get to work, and I assume to get home as well. I've driven him many times and have developed a level of relationship that makes for an easy ride, good conversation and just an overall good feeling that rideshare driving works for me. As it turns out, we have some things in common, which make for a good 15 minute ride that is very relaxing and gets my day going in a positive way.

When driving in a specific area on a regular basis, you will drive some regulars who are a pleasure to pick up and get them on their way; this is one of those times.

Erika (with daughter)

Airport to Home

A nice young lady with a quiet and tired daughter, returning from a long day of traveling from many states away. As our conversation went on, and the topic of this book surfaced, she wanted to share a personal experience she had with another ride some time ago. She had ordered a ride some time ago, when a car pulled up and was similar to the one on the app. The UBER/Lyft app is not always correct, so she was about to get in. Just then, another vehicle pulled up and yelled out, 'are you Erika'. Then the original car driver said, 'you can get in anyway'. This could have been a bad story and was avoided just in time.

Emilee

Home to Work

Typically on early morning rides, it's sorta quiet, with the exception of the radio. Normal chit-chat and that is all. However, this time was different. She talked about where she worked (Veterinary Hospital) and what she did (Duties as assigned). One of her duties was definitely more difficult in the beginning was assisting in euthanasia procedures. At first, very traumatic, but eventually learning to cope with both the animal and the owner(s) has helped her deal with it. The sadness still arises in her every time though. Mentioning that we often get the pet soon after their birth, experience their whole lives with them, then having to see them move on to the next world can be most difficult. Early in the morning, these types of thoughts can certainly get your day going and your mind thinking.

Jason

Restaurant to Hotel

Only a short ride but it was a quick conversation from a traveler in town for only a few days. He mentioned his father passed away just 2 years ago and he's out on his own as the age of 24. His company is paying for the expenses and he's working on a labor job, hoping to experience some of the outside world, since his roots are in Iowa. I wish him good luck.

Cheves

Home to friend's house

Outgoing and smiley person, with a positive outlook and always seems to be in a hurry doing something and/or going somewhere. She says her rest time is when she's in an UBER, but not really, because she's on the phone with her sister and family. Face time, I believe, in another state. Imagine this scenario just ten years ago, awesome, just awesome.

Matt

Hotel to Airport

He is a wood working professional from Arkansas. He's been clean from alcohol for almost 8 years now. The conversation quickly turns to his life experiences. Finding his passion in woodworking some time ago, even though he was studying to become a lawyer and then a therapist, he decided to drop out of school and do what he loves. His decision to change paths was because at the time he was struggling with an alcohol addiction and felt that it would probably be a conflict with those two professions. He started doing some wood working projects and quickly realized how much he loved it. Along the way, he hit his 'rock bottom' with the alcohol addiction, and he refers to that time as his 'enlightment moment' when he realizes there is more to life than the next drink. Now, not only is he loving what he does for a living, he gets paid to speak about his passion; woodworking, and he still has time to work on his own projects as well.

Sondra
College to Train Station

Standoffish, young, a recent college graduate, she is back for Homecoming festivities. She has the sense about her that the world revolves around her, much like a number of young people, until they experience otherwise. I feel bad for her, a lot to learn about life that they just don't teach you in school.

George
Store to Home

As he gets into my car I smell the distinct odor of marijuana, so I know he's been smoking. It's a 15 minute ride, but 3 minutes into it, he says he forgot his bag of lunchmeats, etc. on the sidewalk where he was waiting for me. He immediately offered me $10 to go back, which I would have done anyway, for free. So, we are then driving to his home and of course, I engage in conversation, like every other ride.

And I put on the customer choice of music, or I guess what that may be, either way, it typically is enjoyed by the rider(s). He was very happy with the chosen music and the conversation, and he eventually offered me some of what he was smoking. I refuse as I always do, with any offerings of any sort from any passenger. It's just good practice. So, we get to his home and he tips me another $40 for going back, etc. He exits the car, I start to drive off and I glance in the back seat, just making sure he didn't leave anything behind. I notice a crumpled up bill and I turn around to go give it back. I arrive and he comes out wondering why I returned, finding out why, he gives me the crumpled up $5 bill. All in all, a good trip financially, just for being nice.

Cierra

Friend's house to home

An 18 year old girl, who works at a fast food restaurant, was willing to talk, even early in the morning. Customer service is often times a good conversation, mostly because I can empathize with them on dealing with people. And many people, me included, can oftentimes get so self absorbed with our own lives, that we fail to see or understand the lives of other people in the midst of transacting business. Such is the case with fast food restaurants; there is typically little empathy toward the workers and their plight to provide a quality product in a timely manner. I mention that this book is partly about that, the idea that everyone has a story. And, as human beings, we many times forget that in our daily lives.

Nathan
School to Home

At first glance, a twenty something with tattoos up both arms, ripped jeans, and just putting out a cigarette before entering the car, I had unfortunately allowed my eyes to make the first impression of him. And, of course, I was wrong. Many times I'll listen to symphony music in the car (satellite radio), but usually I switch it before a passenger gets in. This time, I forgot, and so after realizing this I mention that he could listen to any music he would like, and to my surprise, he listens to symphony music very often. He says it calms him down and helps him focus. Hmmm. And then he proceeds to tell me that he's a full-fledged carpenter, now going to school learning how to be an electrician. His short term goal is to graduate and then start flipping houses, where he'll be able to do most of the contracting work himself. Quite forward thinking for a twenty something and I congratulate and encourage him to keep focused and to make it happen. A very encouraging ride for me, hearing about his story and wishing him good luck, as well as a lesson for me, that looks can be deceiving, and once again they have deceived me.

Lori
Work to Home

It's an early morning ping, headed to a regular pick-up for a short ride that I know starts at a fast food restaurant. I'm thinking maybe I should get a breakfast sandwich, I'm sorta hungry. She gets into the car and, as usual, asks how I'm doing. I say, well, and how are you. She then says, with tears, I'm going home to cry. I'm thinking this is not good. She proceeds to tell me she just heard that her mother has stage 3 lung cancer; no chemo or treatment is given for this stage, only medications for pain. And then Lori says that she needs heart surgery for herself and will need to decide to get it now or wait to support her mother. And here I'm deciding to buy a breakfast sandwich or not. Suddenly, I'm not hungry anymore.

Robert & friend
Bar to another bar

Normally, to get an entry in this book, a threshold needs to be met. After thinking for a short time, I felt this was the case for this ride. It's Veterans Day, and the friend on this ride is a decorated veteran, a Major in the Army, and served three tours in Vietnam. At 81 years old, with his wits about him, I'm sure he has many stories to tell, unfortunately, it's not a long ride, so I'm out of luck. I thank him for his service and hope to see him again.

Christine & friend

School to home

Certain groups of people and certain types of people almost never tip when they get rides. That's just the way it is, could be cultural, or it could be just ignorance of the pay scale for drivers. Either way, this was one of those rides to a school. Sometimes it's a teacher, sometimes it's a student. This time it's two students, with one celebrating their 16th birthday. After discussing some details about the school, etc. the topic of grades surfaced. The birthday girl has 3 F's so far, but the parents do not know. Having just gotten her permit to drive, and as we approach the house, she mentions that she might get a new car for her 16th birthday. I tell her that's wishful thinking, but she seems somewhat confident. Well, as we approach her house, parents on the front porch, there is a brand new SUV, wrapped in a red bow, sitting in the driveway. So, there you have it, feel free to fill in the blanks on this story, because there is definitely more to it.

Driver Thoughts

As I mentioned, most of my rides get made aware of the safety measures built into both rideshare applications. These are there for both the driver and the passenger(s). It is the '911 Emergency Assistance' feature.

It amazes me that many people still don't know about this, especially when there are still 'not good' events still happening. Even though drivers go through a screening process; that includes background checks, there is still the possibility of negative actions by those same drivers. So, I make sure that most passengers know of their existence. Plus, it shows that as a driver, I do care about their safety and security when they use the rideshare systems. And, the more I show that I care; I actually do care, the more tips I secure.

Another safety measure that I mention to people is this. If upon entering the vehicle, something just doesn't look or sound right with the driver or the vehicle, do not get in. Cancel the ride, and then request credit on your account from UBER/Lyft. It's better to be safe now, than sorry later.

Allen
Home – Work

He is a local CEO/CFO of two companies and this is my second ride with him. Recently, some bad things have happened and he wished to relate them to me. A close friend's mom passed away from cancer, was told she would live for about a year, then she died in 2 ½ weeks. Basically, a whirlwind, from diagnosis to hospice to a funeral, it all happened very quickly. This friend has very little family, only one sibling. He mentions that meanwhile many people have lots of family around and just don't get along at all. This person apparently could have used more family for consolation and healing. Then, the next story, in a short period of time, another relative of Allen's, committed suicide. Then, shortly after that, his sister gets in a car accident and is hospitalized. All of this occurred in about 5 weeks. This type of story is happening all around us, at any given time, so my prayers go out to him and I'm humbled at how many blessings that I lose track of and forget about on a daily basis.

Tonisha & fiancé
Motel to home

A young couple, who stayed in a motel due to being out the night before at a party; this normally would not meet the threshold to be in this book, but they were very respectful, polite and appreciative of the ride and the amenities I offer. Firstly, they were overjoyed to get bottled water and some mints at no extra charge. A please and thank you sir came along with the offer. Then, I mentioned that I have Excedrin, if they need it. More positive comments about that offer as well. Then, she was sniffling a few times, so I normally offer small packets of Kleenex that come with a Ziploc sandwich bag for the disposal of them. Even though she declined, they were very satisfied with the ride, which is probably why they left a tip a few minutes after the ride.

Brian & Joanna

Winery to Hospital

They are in town for a wedding ceremony and her sister is having a baby back home, about 90 minutes away. It's a breached baby; so I believe there are some possible medical concerns for the health of the mommy and/or the baby. Because they traveled to this area in a car pool, they do not have their car, so taking an UBER ride is their only option to get there as quickly as possible. I drop them off, say a prayer for all of them and go on my way, hoping for the best. I ask them to respond on the app if everything is ok. I find out later, based on their comments about their ride, that everyone is happy and healthy. This is one of those times that I'm glad that I drive.

Cheves San'ta (pronounced Shu/ves Shan ta)
Home to Hair appointment

Sometimes I ask about the origin of a person's name, how it came to be. In this case, the dad was a funny guy, and sometimes drank a lot of alcohol. He also worked on cars, rebuilding, fixing, etc. His favorite was the Chevy. Shortly after mom gave birth in the hospital; it was time to fill out the final paperwork for the name of the newborn. Well, dad had been drinking and being a 'funny' guy, he decided to call her Cheves, after a car manufacturer, Chevy. The passenger admits now it was kinda funny, but definitely a true story.

Kat & daughter
Train station to Hotel

Having grown up in NYC, they moved to Florida for work and lived there for several years. Unfortunately for them, no one told them about the bugs and the size of them. It does take some time to get used to and that's why they determined that many people have screened in porches. So, they are moving back up the coast to Pennsylvania for mom to retire. I mentioned the oddity of that, because typically, people move from PA to Florida to retire, not the other way around. They laughed and went on their way, another satisfied customer.

Joseph & Lisa

Home to Brother's Home

This ride started out as just a normal ride, with the usual 'Hello's' and 'How are you? Scheduled to be a 22 minute ride, there weren't any clues as to what was about to happen.

The conversation between the two passengers was a little loud and centered on family relationships, specifically Joseph's side of the family. With his mother recently passing away, it created some tensions on which family member get's what, etc. etc. Although that's not abnormal, Joseph seemed to not be too happy with the way things were turning out. He started getting louder and obnoxious, so I nicely mentioned that he needs to settle down a bit.

Well, he didn't take to kindly to my words. He proceeded to go back and forth with me about settling down. His girlfriend, Lisa, was trying to calm him down a bit, but to no avail. He then tells me he is going to rip up the back of the seat, and, of course, I tell him that would not be a good idea.

By this point of the ride, I am keeping one eye on him and one eye on the road. We are also now on a highway going 65 miles an hour. He then says he is going to jump out of the window. I mention that the windows are now locked. Then, he wants to jump out through the door, so I lock them.

Within a few moments, I pull over and mention to him, nicely of course, that he will need to get out, settle down, and then I'll continue the ride. He agrees and gets out, then lights up a cigarette on the side of the highway. Before his girlfriend gets out, she hands me a piece of paper with her name and phone number on it, and says, 'If anything happens to me, tell the authorities about this experience.' Wow, I say to myself, did I sign up for this?

The ride then continues, with no other major incident. For the next few days, I check the local media for any reports, none were found.

Amber, husband & daughter

Home to Center City

Amber, a retired military person in the U.S. Navy, and her family were lucky to be together this day. I drove them all to a Christmas festival. The husband is currently in the military, stationed in Guam, and was unexpectedly permitted to come home over the holiday to be with his family. Also, the daughter, living several states away, was also able to be with them as well. So, all in all, just a feel good story from a military family who is not taking their time together for granted. I thanked them for their service and wished them well that evening and a Merry Christmas!

Sally

Home to Bank Parking Lot

A morning ride, about 18 minutes, headed to a parking lot where her boyfriend was found passed out from alcohol and with her stolen car. After receiving a call from the police, Sally smoothed it over with them, no charges filed. Then, during the ride, a phone conversation with the boyfriend's mother, about the incident and apparently, about another one just recently. Hearing bits and pieces of the conversation, not eavesdropping as it was sorta loud; it ended with not nice name calling and a hang up. And here, just before the ride, I was feeling 'woe is me' about our own family tragedy, just a couple years ago. Once again, realizing that not only does everyone have a story, but 'special' stories are happening all of the time, even if our own seems to get better.

Shawn

Home to Bird Seller to Home

A nice guy going to buy another bird for his home, this turned into a funny story. As the conversation goes on, he mentions how cool it is that the birds fly around in his home, not stuck in a small cage. He has a small rancher but it's still more flying around than most birds kept as pets. He goes on to say that he doesn't believe that birds should be kept in a cage. Then, I say, jokingly and sarcastically, 'really, then let them fly outside'. 'You just have them in a bigger cage.' He laughs and says, 'you know, you're right.'

Dr. Chin

Train Station to Hospital Interview

This was a 24 year old doctor from Princeton, NJ who was born and raised in India. She is going on her 14th interview for her eventual residency, which leads up to becoming an actual doctor. Having finished her schooling ahead of schedule for the average person, she is very focused on her mission in life. Also, she is an active Rotarian, which is not just an ordinary volunteer association. Being a Rotarian requires time, effort and at least, a little financial commitment. It's an organization usually represented by older citizens than someone in their middle 20's. She has a world view of things, which is also uncommon, so I let her know that. She spoke of a terrible flood in India, where the media focused on all of the terrible events that unfolded, but never spoke about the human mobilization of resources of all kinds to help all of the people involved. She says it's typical of the media to have an agenda and to not report the good human sides of such tragic events. I agreed, wished her well, and dropped her off at her interview location.

Driver Thoughts

Each passenger gets to provide a review for the driver after each ride. Most don't; some give a generic review, but some actually put their own words into the system for the driver and future riders to read.

In the beginning, I really looked forward to them, a confidence trip of sorts, and to make sure I'm providing the best service possible. Later on, I've not taken it as serious, mostly because it has nothing to do with how much money is made driving people around. It would be nice if the major rideshare companies provided some incentives to achieve high ratings, but, the bottom line for them, is that they just don't care. And that includes the driver and the passenger. It's sometimes hard to explain that to people, especially since the casual user of the service simply thinks it's a great idea and has helped everyone.

The reality that the rideshare companies are just about the money, will be revealed within the next few years. Because both companies went public within the last year, they now have to answer to stockholders. And it's not just about the money each company is losing, but also how they operate their day to day business. I expect this industry to still exist but to change in ways that may not make everyone happy, for both drivers and passengers.

Dylan

Home to Work

Having slept in past his normal work start time, he was very chatty for a short ride. He said he spends about $100 per week on ridesharing which leaves him about $500 per week to spend on everything else. At 22 years old, he is trying to make it happen. He doesn't have all of the answers, but knows working hard and long hours may be one of them.

Alex

Garage to Garage (long trip)

An interesting story from this 29 year old; graduated from Penn State University and got his Masters from a Philadelphia college and is now working on his doctorate. Looking to become a doctor, and starting a family at the same time, it was going to be one or the other due to time constraints. The family won. He now owns and operates a trucking company and trucking repair shop with his brother in the Northeastern U.S. With no regrets, he feels he is now too old to go back and become a doctor. He has enough money now to finance the finishing of his education to become a doctor but between the family and the family business his desire for that dream seems to be in the past. Sometimes life gets in the way of our dreams in ways we never saw coming, such as in this case.

Steve

Coffee shop to Train Station

This was a long ride and somewhat emotional. Shawn is on his way to a rehab facility and this is his story. Originally from South Florida, mom thinks he is currently in a rehab facility. He avoids calling her back so she doesn't worry as much. I suspect by his conversation that she is one of the few people who still care about him. But this ride to the train station is being paid by a local coffee shop owner; another person who cares.

Shawn is an ex-youth pastor that has been in and out of rehab for years. Near death experiences; emergency room visits; etc. etc. etc. It is the typical addiction path of an individual, although it's still tragic, just more common than most people know or would want to know.

I related to him a personal experience which caused him to open up even more. He knows it is a journey to recovery and the path is up to him; but relying on the Lord for strength is his great hope. He does all the right things in AA, he says all the right things to his support groups, but the real challenge is the day to day living. I congratulate and encourage him to keep the faith. He exits the vehicle and I say my traditional prayer for him as I do for most passengers.

Hillary & friend
Home to Christmas Party

Nice people going to a Christmas party being held late due to inclement weather. It's at a cool place and I mention how nice that is for the company to do that. They counter with the idea that the company is actually really cheap. They say the company pays for the first three drinks and I say, 'that's awesome'. Then the friend says, 'No, they are actually very, very cheap. If they saw a dime in your throat, they would try to pull a quarter out of your ***'. I laugh, then let them out of the vehicle, and wish them well.

Isaiah & 4 friends
Home to Bar

Because my vehicle only holds 5 total occupants, this was a dilemma solved by the hatch in the back. I said someone could ride in the hatch and they proceeded to choose the lucky passenger. It's not that bad, there is a pillow in the hatch and it's not air tight, so a person can still breathe. Like many rides, especially longer ones like this, I let them choose the music and even how loud. Going out with your friends to a bar, the fun can start before getting there. So, the music is turned up and every 5-10 minutes, I turn it down ask the guy in the hatch if he's ok, after his response, the music gets turned up again. I mention to the others, that they should buy him his first drink and they agree. So, we get to the bar, a fairly big parking lot, and there are lots of people walking in. Somehow, we all ended up in a semi-circle at the back of the car as I open the hatch and out jumps the hatch back passenger. I can only imagine what other people thought as they witnessed this scene.

Johnathan

Motel to Office

Having flown in from Boise, Idaho, I simply asked, 'Why here?' This is a small town and he lives a long way from here. One of things that used to surprise me was how far some people go to get here for reasons I never knew or would have suspected. It turns out, there is a world renowned expert in parachuting that resides here and uses our very small airport for training. This is just another reason why I'm happy to have had the experience of ridesharing in our small town.

Timothy
Vet – Home – Bar

One of my regulars; not sure why he seems to need rides, there are always parked cars in the driveway. But, asking questions like that is not always a good thing and sometimes it can bring up negative vibes and that's never good for a good ride and potential tips.

Corinne
Home to Work

I could instantly see she had a lot on her mind, and was on a mission. I offered a free water and mint, like I do for every passenger. She was most thankful and said she really needed it at this time. Offering amenities is good especially since as a driver we never know the story going on, but most times there is one and if we can be a positive part of that, it can be a good thing. Plus, like this drive, there was a tip, just for being nice.

Valerie & friend

Train Station to Hotel

These two are only in town for a day; they've come all the way from Manhattan, NYC. After they experience my free water and mints, they immediately talk about some other driver experiences they've had. One driver would play his flute while stopped at a red light; another driver just would not stop talking and was very annoying. Another driver handed them a business card that simply said, 'Driver' on the front of it. So, just as drivers experience many different types of passengers, it works the opposite way as well.

Carrie

Boyfriend's house to Bar

I pulled up to the address on the app and saw a truck pulling out of the driveway; I waved them out so I can pull in. Then, the truck waited in the street and was watching me. The passenger cuts across a yard to get in my vehicle and we take off. It turns out; she put the wrong address in for the pick-up. After driving for a while, a drive needs to pay attention after arriving at the pick-up location,. The GPS system is not perfect. Most people do not like strange cars coming into their driveway. And I always fear that someone will come out with a shotgun or some weapon of choice and ask me, what are you doing here?

Jasmyn
Home to Boyfriend's Home

Conversation started with her name being given by her dad who had a dream that she should be named Jasmyn. No explanation as to why, other than a dream. Commenting nicely on a name often times opens up a good dialogue right from the start. She eventually revealed an experience of a bad ridesharing experience. A scary looking guy picked her up, played weird music and drove around aimlessly while going toward her destination. He tried to 'hit' on her with lewd comments and suggestions. After the ride she reported him to the ridesharing company. Although that's the right thing to do, it's not likely that there will be any ramifications for the driver. The ridesharing companies, in general, just do not care. They say they do, but their actions do not reflect that sentiment. My suggestion to her and others is to refuse the ride, if possible. Or end the ride sooner and secure another driver. It's better to be safe now than sorry later.

Driver Thoughts

There are many new and unexpected happenings with driving for the ridesharing companies and one of them was and is concerning safety, particularly for me.

Originally, I thought of carrying a firearm, just because you never know who is going to come into the vehicle, but I never did. Many times it's not even the person requesting the ride that is in the car. And while drivers undergo a thorough background check for felonies, DUI's, traffic violations or any criminal history, this is not the case for passengers. So, I considered that a risk, then, and still do. However, driving in small towns, I believe the risk is much less than the larger cities. Plus, I rarely drive after 9PM at night, so, the additional alcohol effect is minimized.

Even with this knowledge, there are still drivers and passengers who will act in very unprofessional or unlawful ways.

Very few passengers realize that when they downloaded the application to their phone, before their first ride, they agreed to certain terms and conditions. These include, but are not limited to, using profanity, unruly behavior, physically touching the driver in any way, etc. etc.

Paul
Home to Work

Another regular rider, a good guy, active in the community and we always have a good conversation. Normally, different topics are discussed as well, which keeps it interesting. Typically, I believe that in some ways, as a driver, I can be therapeutic for a passenger. Meaning they can say things without any negative feedback, but mostly sympathy and only constructive criticism when they seek it. But, this is one of those times where the passenger is therapeutic for me, but he doesn't realize that and that's the beauty of it.

Allen
Home to Work

2nd ride with this passenger, he's another good guy with many stories to tell. He is growing 5 orange trees in his basement, yes, he's is growing oranges in his basement. Using different growing methods, he is experimental in the ways of horticulture. And, he currently has many connections in the book publishing world and has offered to help me with the publishing, marketing, etc. I end up using other resources for such matters, but it was nice of him to offer his services. This is one of the reasons driving in a small town is special, the people are different, and mostly in a good way.

Steven

Work to Home to Work

Picking him up at his first job, then to his home, and then I'm to take him to his second job. He asked if I could wait 5-10 minutes after the first stop and I agreed. It's over 12 minutes of wait time and it doesn't sound like much. But, ridesharing is different than a taxi in this way. When we need to wait, we lose money. It costs the passenger only $1.50 every 10 minutes, unlike a taxi where it's a lot more per minute. Normally I don't mind as I have many things to occupy my time. But, that is not the case for all drivers; I've heard more than once of drivers just driving off after the first stop on a multiple stop trip. I usually explain why to customers, but most don't understand. Many passengers just think we are part of the public transit system and that we get all or most of the fare; but that's just not the case. Unfortunately the major rideshare companies do not want the passengers to see what the driver actually gets paid as it might change the opinion of them.

George
Pharmacy to Home

Sometimes riders do not smell the greatest, so it's good to have an air freshener in your vehicle. I use a febreze version attached to the vent, seems to work well. Also, a good smelling car that is also clean looking can increase the possibility of a tip for your service.

Nishigandha
College Dorm to Class

Short trip for a college student that is sometimes annoying, mostly because it's only $3.89 for the ride. It is cold outside and walking for 5 to 10 minutes is just too much for some people. Well, that's the nice way of thinking about it.

Issandra
Home to Work

She is a high school student and I quickly realize she is focused on her future. Working 2 jobs and taking an online anatomy class, just to get a head start on her college career at Fordham University. It's refreshing to interact with a young person with this many aspirations.

Nairobi & two children
Home to Daycare to Work

Mom and her 2 children, on a snowy winter morning, are starting their day, only a few weeks before Christmas. Both children seem good natured and loved. Mom mentioned she needs to drop them off at daycare and then go to work. I did not ask if she put in the multiple destinations and when we get to the day care, I finish the trip per the application. When she returns to the car, I mention she can either pay me cash by getting the normal fare charge and rounding down or to order a new ride through the app. The fare would be $16 so I say $10 is fine; but she insists on $15. As we arrive, she begins to get the money out and I say, just keep it, Merry Christmas! Without another word, I drive off. It's my good deed for the day and well worth it as I know they could use that money better than me during this time of year.

Shaniece
Grocery Store to Home

Picking someone up at the grocery store is typically one of the worst trips for a rideshare driver;

for several reasons. When people go to the grocery store, many times they spend more than they intended and that normally translates into no tip. Plus, it's almost always a short ride, maybe $3 or $4. Also, if they are not nice and treat the driver like its public transportation, that makes it even worse. In this case, she was very nice, but no tip and $3.87 for the ride. If it's about the money, then this type of ride will contribute to a driver not driving anymore.

Final Words

I have thoroughly enjoyed this ridesharing experience for a couple of years. It has been quite a journey, though, especially remembering when I first started and the evolution of my perception of driving.

It's not for everyone, for a multitude of reasons. First of all, many people feel they can drive for a day or two on the weekends and make hundreds of dollars. It typically does not work that way, unless you are a lucky person and have gotten some long rides.

Another reason many drivers start and quit driving just as fast, is that they fail to approach this venture like a business. For instance, just like in your own business, if it works, keep doing it; if not, change your actions until it does work. If you are not making enough money, maybe you need to drive in a different location or at different times.

One reason I kept driving after a week or two is because I've been blessed to receive a high rate of tips. My sales background kicked in gear to make each trip the best it could be for each ride; regardless of the passenger or how far they are going. That alone doesn't guarantee tips, but it sure helped. Having water bottles, life saver mints, small packets of tissues, Excedrin and Tylenol available can make a difference. Every drive did not partake in all of that, but when they did, most of the time it was unexpected and most appreciated.

About the Author

Everyone has a story and here's mine. I grew up in a small town, moved away to go to college, lived in Europe for 5 months, moved to a large city, met my wife, then moved back to a small town to raise a family.

Everyone has a story to tell and that is one of the beneficial side effects of writing this book; there are plenty of stories. When I began driving, I realized that people were telling me their story and I started writing them down to form this first book. It started with emotional hard luck stories from real people with daily trials and tribulations that no one hears about because they keep it to themselves. The book then evolved to include funny, interesting and thought provoking details about regular, everyday people.

I hope you enjoy reading this book as much as I've enjoyed writing it.

www.realstoriesfromaridesharedriver.com

Made in the USA
Elizabethtown, PA
March 2020

ISBN

9781787233102

Milton Keynes UK
Ingram Content Group UK Ltd.
UKHW021044131123
432477UK00015B/919

9 781787 233102